Includes Revised Order of Mass +

Called to Serve

A Guidebook for Altar Servers

(Revised and Updated)

Father Albert M. Nevins, M.M.

Our Sunday Visitor Publishing Division
Our Sunday Visitor, Inc.
Huntington, Indiana 46750

Excerpts from the new English translation of the *Roman Missal,* © 2010 by the International Commission on English in the Liturgy Corporation. All rights reserved. With the exception of short excerpts for critical reviews, no part of this book may be reproduced in any manner whatsoever without permission in writing from the publisher. Write:
Our Sunday Visitor Publishing Division
Our Sunday Visitor, Inc.
200 Noll Plaza
Huntington, Indiana 46750

ISBN-13: 978-1-59276-594-2 (Inventory No. X876)

Cover design by Tyler Ottinger, photo from Design Pics
Illustrations by DeWayne Salter, Jr.
Photographs: Thinkstock page 5, W.P. Wittman Limited pages 7, 11, 32, 38, 41, OSV file photo page 24
Revision Consultants: Rev. George T.M. Hafemann, Brian MacMichael, Johan van Parys

PRINTED IN THE UNITED STATES OF AMERICA

Contents

"I'll Take You!"

Bobby's first day at the new school had gone well — so far. But recess would really be the test. Bobby had been in town for only three days. He didn't know any of these kids.

Over by the baseball diamond, a group was gathering. They were choosing up sides for a quick game. "They'll never choose me!" Bobby thought to himself as he walked slowly toward the playing field. "They don't even know me."

Bobby was only a few steps from the small crowd when he heard one of the captains call out in his direction, "I'll take you — the new kid." Bobby could hardly believe it. As he jogged over to where the captain was standing, he tried to contain the smile on his face. He felt terrific.

Like Bobby, you have just been chosen. You've been asked to become a part of a very special group of people: your parish's altar servers. Perhaps it was one of the parish priests who made the invitation to you. But keep this in mind: It was God who made the call. God wants you to play a very important part in the life of your parish. He wants you to help your parish worship by being a server. There is much to learn ahead. But for now, it's important to realize that you have received a call from God to serve. God does not call strangers. He calls friends. And he has called you, as Scripture says, "by your name."

God has been calling people to serve him for centuries. There are the great leaders whose names we know: Abraham, Moses, David, Mary. Even Jesus himself was called by his Father. There are also the millions of people whose names we do not know. But God knew their names and he called them by name. Now it is your turn. God wants you at his altar to help the celebrations go well so as to promote the spiritual well-being of his people as they come together in prayer. This is not the first time God has called you, and it will not be the last. But it is a very special call. Respond to it with enthusiasm. Give it everything you've got!

2

The Mass

For Catholics, nothing is more important than the Mass. It is the heart and soul of our worship of God. It is the celebration that gives us the strength we need to live a Christian life. Because of its importance, the Church places a serious obligation on all its members to participate in the Mass each Sunday and holy day.

Thus each Sunday the Christian community comes together to give worship to the Eternal Father and our Lord, Jesus Christ. Of all things Catholics do, nothing is more important than celebrating Mass together. In your call to ministry, you will assist at other services, but none is as important as your service at Mass as one of the leaders of the community.

The Mass makes real and present the Last Supper, when Jesus instituted the Eucharist and told his followers, "Do this in memory of me." Although the Mass is a mystery, we believe that bread and wine become the Body and Blood of Jesus Christ because Jesus told us this is so. Some descriptions will help us to understand it better.

First and foremost, the Mass is a sacrifice. The idea of sacrifice to God is at the very heart of faith. The Bible tells us how Abel and Cain, the sons of Adam, offered sacrifice to God. Abraham, whom the liturgy calls "our father in faith," was prepared to offer to God his only son, Isaac. The people of the Old Testament through their priests sacrificed lambs and goats to God. Jesus offered his Father a sacrifice: himself. Jesus promised us that "when we eat this bread and drink this cup," he would continue his great sacrifice until he comes again in glory.

The Mass is a memorial. It is an event that helps people to remember. The most important event, the one remembered at every Mass, is the death and resurrection of Jesus Christ. We also remember through the readings other great deeds God has done for his people.

The Mass is also a sacred meal called the Eucharist (from the Greek *eucharístia*, meaning "thanksgiving"). In the Mass we give thanks for all God has done for us, and we all eat the same food — "the Bread of life and the Chalice of salvation" (Eucharistic Prayer I). Jesus has told us that this bread and wine are his Body and Blood (read John 6:53-55). So, in this sacred meal, we believe that Jesus' life, death, and resurrection are continued for all of us through our celebration, begun at the Last Supper.

The way in which Mass is celebrated has developed over almost two thousand years. The early Christians called it "the Breaking of the Bread." Despite its development, two elements have always been the same: listening to God's word in Scripture and partaking of the consecrated Eucharistic meal. Today we refer to these elements as the Liturgy of the Word and the Liturgy of the Eucharist. Following is the basic outline of the Mass, which you should learn well.

The Order of Mass

A. The Introductory Rites
✠ Entrance *Procession*. Usually from the back of the church down the center aisle. Usual participants: cross-bearer, other servers, lector, concelebrants, deacon, celebrant.

✠ *Greeting*. By the celebrant.

✠ *Blessing and Sprinkling of/with Holy Water*. This is often done during the Easter season. When it is done, the Penitential Act is omitted.

✠ *Penitential Act*. This can be done in various ways. We'll learn the necessary prayers and responses later. This may include the *Kyrie ("Lord, have mercy")*.

✠ *Gloria*. This hymn is said or sung on all Sundays outside of Lent and Advent, and on great feasts. You should memorize this hymn.

✠ *Opening Prayer*. Also called the "Collect" prayer, because it "collects" all the people's opening prayers into one prayer said by the priest.

B. The Liturgy of the Word
✠ *First Reading*. Read by lector, usually from the Old Testament.

✠ *Responsorial Psalm*. Usually led by the cantor but may be recited. It is never omitted.

✠ *Second Reading*. Also by the lector. (On most weekdays there is no second reading.)

✠ *Gospel Acclamation*. The cantor sings it first and the congregation repeats. It may be omitted when not sung, but should never be recited.

✠ *Gospel*. Taken from one of the four Gospels, it is read by the priest or deacon. It is good to learn the responses to the readings.

✠ *Homily*. By the priest or deacon, explaining the Scriptures and how they impact our lives.

✠ *Profession of Faith (Creed)*. Said on Sundays and certain feasts. All join in this declaration of beliefs. We'll learn the words later.

✠ *Prayer of the Faithful*. You lead the people in response to each petition.

C. The Liturgy of the Eucharist

✠ *Preparation of the Gifts*. This is also called the offertory. Sometimes the cross-bearer goes down and leads the people bearing the gifts to the altar. Meanwhile, other servers prepare the altar, then accompany the priest to receive the gifts. There is a prayer at the end, which we will learn shortly.

✠ *Eucharistic Prayer.* There are various Eucharistic prayers, but the responses you need to know are pretty much the same for each. Here are parts of the Eucharistic Prayer you should know: the preface dialogue; the *Sanctus*, or Holy, Holy, Holy; the words of institution (also called the consecration); the Mystery of Faith, the Great Amen.

✠ *Communion Rite*. This part begins with the Lord's Prayer (Our Father) and ends with the Prayer after Communion. There are several prayers you should know here.

D. The Concluding Rites

Brief announcements may be made here.

✠ *Greeting and Final Blessing*. There are varied forms for this, to which everyone responds.

✠ *Dismissal.* The priest sends the congregation out to serve God and the world. The ministers leave in procession, departing the altar area in the order in which they entered.

Since servers are important ministers of the celebration, you should be very familiar with the order of Mass. You have to know well the things you do so that they are second nature to you. This leaves you free to concentrate on your involvement in prayer.

The remaining chapters of *Called to Serve* will require study. Remember, the better you know your duties, the easier it will be for you to fulfill your duties as a leader of prayer.

3

The Server: "Who, Me...Lead Prayer?"

Young people have been serving Mass from the earliest centuries. They have helped to get things ready: assisting the priest with vestments, lighting candles, carrying the books used at Mass, ringing bells, saying prayers in practically every known language. They have been getting up early in the morning, staying up late at night. Of utmost importance, however, is not really the things they do but the example they give.

More than anything else, the server is a leader of prayer. Servers help people to pray. So, servers must ask themselves, "What is prayer?"

To begin with, prayer is listening, listening to God. During the Mass, there's much to be listened to. There's music, the priest's prayers, the people's prayers, and especially the words of Scripture. All the things servers have to do during Mass cannot be a distraction to their listening. Remember, the server is a part of the celebration. The server is not like a waiter in a restaurant who stands off to the side and only helps out occasionally. A waiter is not usually a part of the dinner celebration, but the server is; the server is a part of the celebration, listening all the time. This is one way you pray: by listening.

Another part of prayer is, of course, responding. At Mass the community responds in prayer and song. In our prayers and songs, praise and thanks are given to God for all the great things he has done. So, unless you are doing something that makes it impossible, you should be praying and singing whenever it is called for.

People will see you participating through your listening, praying, and singing. This will help them to feel more comfortable about praying and singing themselves. This is your first leadership job: to be a leader of prayer.

The Ministers at Mass

It takes quite a few people to celebrate Mass well. In larger parishes there may be as many as forty or fifty people ministering (if you count the choir). In smaller parishes, there are far fewer. "To minister" means "to serve." So all of these people serve the community, helping them worship well.

Celebrant — This is the priest who presides over the celebration of the Mass. Sometimes, at what is called a concelebrated Mass, there may be more than one priest. But the one who presides is the one you should be concerned most about. Mostly, your job is to help him.

Deacon — Depending on whether you have a deacon at your parish, this person may or may not be part of your team. When present, the deacon usually proclaims the Gospel, prepares the gifts for Eucharist, helps to distribute Communion, and may preach.

Altar Servers (Acolytes) — You, and what this book is about.

Lector — This is the person who reads the first two readings. There may be two lectors: one for the first reading, one for the second. In some parishes, this person also leads the responsorial psalm and the intercessions.

Cantor — This is the leader of song. This person helps lead the people in singing the hymns, acclamations, and frequently the responsorial psalm.

Director of Music Ministries — This person is in charge of all the music in the parish. Frequently this person is also the choir director or organist.

Choir Members and Musicians — These people sing sacred music and play the various instruments that lead and accompany the music for the Mass. Choir members are also ministers.

Commentator — This person makes announcements and helps the congregation follow the order of Mass. The lector may fill this role.

Ushers/Ministers of Hospitality — These people greet the community as they arrive for Mass. They try to be sure that everyone is comfortably seated. They take up the collection at Mass.

Sacristan — This person usually works before Mass, making sure that everything that is needed is where it belongs. You may be asked to help with this work.

Extraordinary Ministers of Holy Communion — These ministers are specially trained to assist the priest and deacon in distributing Holy Communion. In some parishes they are part of the procession.

Things to Know About

Because the Mass is such an ancient prayer, there are many elements that have become a part of the celebration. Servers must be familiar with these terms. You should know what these things are, how they are used, and where they are kept. Spaces are provided after some of these descriptions below. These spaces will allow you to write in where the object is stored and any other information that your leader feels is necessary.

SERVICE BOOKS These are the special books used during the liturgy.

Roman Missal (Sacramentary) — This is a large book that contains all the words and prayers the priest uses during Mass, except the readings. At times, you will be asked to carry and hold the Missal for him so that he can pray from it. Write here where the book is stored.

_____

_____

Lectionary — This book contains all the Scripture readings for Mass.

_____

_____

Book of the Gospels — This book contains the Gospel readings (taken from the Lectionary). It is usually carried in the entrance procession by the deacon (or the lector if no deacon is present). It is usually placed on the altar, then carried to the ambo at the Gospel.

_____

_____

Ordo — This book tells what feast day it is, what the readings are, and what the proper color of the day is. It is usually found in the vesting sacristy.

Hymnal — This book contains the hymns and psalms for Mass. You should keep this book near you so that you can sing whenever possible.

(*Note:* Only official books should be used during Mass. Unless absolutely necessary, substitutes, such as a monthly missal, should not be used at the altar.)

THE SANCTUARY The sanctuary is that space at the front of the church within which the central action of the Mass takes place. The word means "holy place." In most churches this space is somewhat elevated. There are many things in the sanctuary with which you should be familiar. At the end of this section is a blank page for you to draw the sanctuary of your church and label the things in the sanctuary (described below), showing where they are placed in your church.

Main Altar — This is the large table usually located in the middle of the sanctuary. Most of the action of the Liturgy of the Eucharist takes place near the main altar.

Altar Cloth — This is the white tablecloth for the main altar.

Ambo (Pulpit) — This is the place where the readings and the Gospel are proclaimed, and the homily given. In many churches there is also a lectern (simple reading stand) to the side from which announcements are made and used by the cantor and commentator.

Credence Table — A small table, on which is kept the *Roman Missal* and chalice (until transferred to the altar after the Prayer of the Faithful). The wine, water (unless brought forward during the Preparation of the Gifts), and finger dish and towel are kept here. Sometimes the sacred vessels are purified here after Communion.

Candles — There may be variations here. Ordinarily, there are candles on each side of the altar, lighted before Mass by servers, or carried in with the procession. Candles might also be lighted before Mass on each side of the tabernacle.

Paschal Candle — The paschal candle, used from the Easter Vigil through Pentecost Sunday, is placed near the altar or ambo during the Easter season and is lit for all Masses to commemorate the Risen Christ among us. It is also used for funerals and baptisms.

Cruets — The pitcherlike vessels containing the water and wine are kept on the credence table or placed on the gift table.

Processional Cross — This is the cross/crucifix mounted on a long pole that is carried at the head of the procession; it may also be carried in procession when the gifts are brought forward. It is usually kept in a stand at the side of the sanctuary.

Tabernacle — This is the safelike container in which the Eucharist is kept. It is located in various places in different churches, but usually behind the main altar. Your leader will teach you the proper reverences to it. Hosts are sometimes taken from here at Communion time.

Bells — The bells may be rung at the consecration. Your leader will give you instructions on what is done in your parish. The bells are usually kept near the servers' places. If used, learn how to ring them properly.

OUR SANCTUARY (On this page, with the help of your leader, draw a sketch of your sanctuary. Show where all the items mentioned above are located and label them.)

VESTMENTS In the earliest days of the Church, Mass was usually celebrated in people's homes. Congregations were rather small then, sometimes because those found practicing Christian worship were in danger of persecution or even death. The priest and other ministers wore what everybody else wore. As years passed, the Church community grew and worship became more public. Sometimes there were thousands of people in attendance at Mass. People had to be able to tell easily who the various ministers were. As a result, special garments were adopted for the various ministers at Mass. The vestments we use today are thus very ancient in origin, many being adapted from ancient Roman vesture, and carrying special symbolism. They help us tell easily who is doing what at Mass.

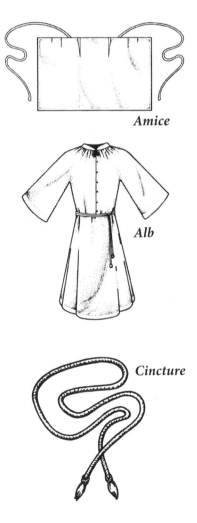

Amice

Alb

Cincture

Amice — This is a rectangular piece of cloth with two long ribbons attached to the top corners. The priest puts it over his shoulders, tucking it in around the neck to hide his cassock and collar. It is worn whenever the alb does not completely cover the ordinary clothing at the neck. It is tied around the waist. The priest puts this on himself.

Alb — Because of their baptism, this long, white, dresslike vestment can be used by all liturgical ministers. It is helpful for the server to stand behind the minister, when he vests, to see that the alb hangs properly in the back.

Cincture — This is a long cord used for fastening some albs at the waist. It holds the loose-fitting type of alb in place and is used to adjust it to the proper length. The cincture is usually white, although the liturgical color of the day may be used.

Stole

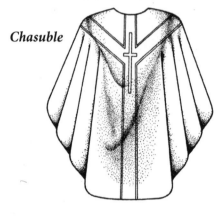

Chasuble

Dalmatic

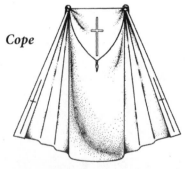

Cope

Stole — A stole is a long cloth "scarf," often ornately decorated, of the same color and style as the chasuble. According to the manner in which it is worn, it is a mark of the office of priest or deacon. A priest wears it around the neck, letting it hang down in front. A deacon wears it over his left shoulder and fastened at his right side like a sash. (There is a smaller stole, white on one side and purple on the other, which some priests use for the anointing of the sick and the Sacrament of Penance.)

Chasuble — The chasuble is the sleeveless outer vestment, slipped over the head, and which hangs down from the shoulders and covers the stole and alb. It is the proper Mass vestment of the priest, and its color varies according to the feast and liturgical season. The server, standing behind, should see that it hangs properly during vesting.

Other vestments used in liturgical ceremonies are:

Dalmatic — The dalmatic is a loose-fitting robe with open sides and wide sleeves worn by the deacon. It takes its color from the liturgical feast.

Cope — A capelike vestment that is put on over the shoulders and hangs to the ankles, it is open in the front and clasped at the neck. The priest frequently wears it in processions, at Eucharistic Benediction, and in other services. Copes may be found in any of the liturgical colors.

Benediction Veil — Also known as a humeral veil, this is a long, narrow, shawl-like vestment used at Benediction and in processions in which the Blessed Sacrament is carried.

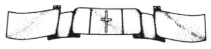

Benediction Veil

Server's Alb — This is a vestment used by servers in place of the cassock and surplice. It is similar to the priest's alb, but sometimes has a hood. It is usually fastened around the waist with a cincture, often in the liturgical color. Make sure your alb is neither too long (which can cause you to trip during Mass) nor too short.

Server's Alb

Cassock — A long outer garment worn by clerics and servers. It is usually black, but for servers red or white cassocks may be worn for special feasts.

Cassock

Surplice — This is a wide-sleeved garment, slipped over the head, covering the shoulders, and coming down below the hips. It is worn over the cassock for services in which the alb is not necessary.

Surplice

ALTAR VESSELS Altar vessels are frequently called "sacred" because they have a distinctive role in our worship.

Chalice — The large cup used at Mass to hold the wine that becomes the Blood of Christ.

Chalice

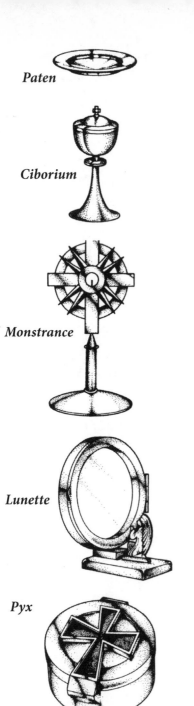

Paten

Ciborium

Monstrance

Lunette

Pyx

Communion Paten

Paten — This is a saucerlike dish hat usually matches the chalice with vhich it is used. It holds the bread that ecomes the Body of Christ.

Ciborium — This is a cuplike vessel usually large) with a lid. It contains he hosts that will be used for Holy Communion. It is also used to reserve he Blessed Sacrament in the tabernacle.

Monstrance — This is a large, ornate vessel used to hold the Blessed Sacrament for Benediction and Eucharistic processions.

Luna, or *Lunette* — A thin, circular receptacle, having a glass face that holds the consecrated Host used at Benediction. It slides into the monstrance on a track.

Pyx — 1. A metal case in which the lunette is kept in the tabernacle.
2. A small round case in which Holy Communion used for sick calls is carried and taken to the sick and homebound.

Communion Paten — This is a plate with a handle that a server may use to catch Communion crumbs. The server stands at the side of the person distributing Holy Communion and holds the paten under the chin of the one receiving when the person receiving Communion does not receive it in the hand.

Large Paten, or *Bread Plate* — It is becoming more common to use a large paten in place of the ciborium. On this is placed the bread that will be consecrated for Communion. This paten is ordinarily brought up in procession at the presentation of the gifts. It may be the duty of a server to see that this paten, with the bread, is brought to the rear of the church before Mass. If this task falls to you, be careful not to drop any bread while going down the aisle.

Large Paten or Bread Plate

Flagon, or *Decanter* — This is the bottle, pitcher, or carafelike vessel used to hold the wine that will be consecrated at Mass for the Communion of the people. It is filled before Mass and brought to the rear of the church for the procession that will bring the gifts forward.

Flagon or Decanter

Communion Cups/Chalices — These chalices are less ornate than the chalice a priest uses, but are also made of metal. They are used when the people receive the Precious Blood from the cup during Holy Communion. They are usually kept on the credence table and brought to the altar at the preparation of the altar and gifts.

Communion Cup

MISCELLANEOUS Other items used at Mass include the following:

Pall — This is the stiff square white cover that may be placed over the paten when it is on the chalice and over the chalice during Mass to protect its contents.

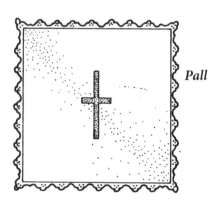

Pall

Chalice Veil

Chalice Veil — This is the large square cloth, matching the vestments of the day, that may be used to cover the chalice before the presentation of the gifts.

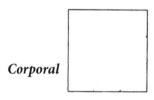

Corporal

Corporal — A square white linen cloth, usually starched, on which are placed the vessels containing the bread and wine during Mass. It is folded into a small square about the size of the pall. When unfolded, it is placed on top of the altar cloth to catch any Eucharistic particles that may fall. It is also used at the tabernacle at Benediction or when the Blessed Sacrament is exposed.

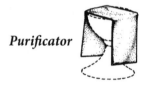

Purificator

Purificator — This is a triple-folded rectangular white cloth used to cleanse the chalice and to dry the celebrant's fingers after the post-Communion ablution (washing). In setting up the chalice, the purificator is placed over the top of the cup, beneath the paten. A purificator almost always has a small red cross in its center.

Finger Towel

Lavabo Bowl *and* **Finger Towel** — A small dish and towel used by the priest to wash and dry his fingers after they have been washed during the preparation of the gifts. It is kept with the cruets and sometimes brought forward with them. The water cruet is typically used to pour water into this bowl.

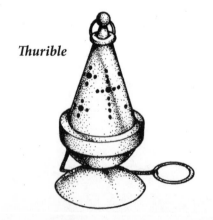

Thurible

Thurible — The metal container extended from a chain (or chains) in which charcoal and incense are burned for liturgical ceremonies. It may have a lid that can be raised, and may also come with a stand on which it can hang when not being used. It is sometimes called a censer.

Boat

Boat — This is a small metal container that holds the incense to be put into the thurible. It has a cover and comes with a small spoon. Frequently shaped like a boat, it is a symbol of the Church, the barque of Peter.

Aspergillum — Also called the holy water sprinkler, it is a perforated metal ball or tube on a handle that holds the holy water used by the priest to sprinkle the faithful or items to be blessed. It is often kept in a small metal bucket (with a handle) that holds holy water.

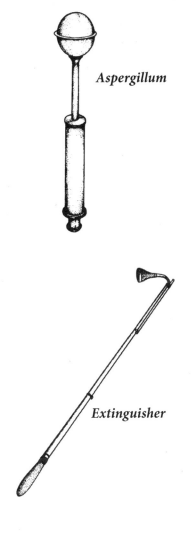

Aspergillum

Extinguisher/snuffer — While this tool takes its name from putting out candles, it is also used to light them. It is a polelike instrument with a tube at one side on the top with a retractable wick for lighting candles. The server using it should have enough wick exposed so that the flame will not go out until all candles are lit. Then the tab should be used to retract the wick and put the flame out. The other side of the top is a cup for extinguishing the candles. Often the server cannot see over the top of the candle, so practice is needed.

Extinguisher

6

Actions to Learn

Beginning golfers have a lot of things to worry about. They must be concerned with how their feet are placed, how straight their arm is on the backswing, whether or not their head is down and eyes are on the ball. A professional golfer does not have to think of these things. Through practice, good posture and swing come naturally.

So it should be with serving Mass. The various actions we do may be a bit forced and stiff at first, but through doing them correctly each time, and practicing them, they should become second nature to us — things we do naturally and easily without thinking. Remember, servers are "public people": they are seen. Your actions should be neither sloppy nor rigid.

FOLDED HANDS

Teachers of public speaking say that one of the most difficult things to teach students is what to do with their hands. The more a speaker becomes conscious of his hands, the bigger the problem can become.

Servers should not have this worry. They have a simple rule: *When the hands are not in use, they should be folded — except when the server is seated (see Page 29).*

Here is how you fold your hands:
1. Put palm against palm.
2. Put the left thumb over the right knuckle.
3. Put the right thumb over the left hand to form an X.
4. Keep the elbows near the body.
5. Make sure that the hands are held in front of the chest with fingers pointing up at a 45-degree angle.

Hands should be folded in this manner whenever you are walking, genuflecting, or kneeling.

SIGN OF THE CROSS

The story is told that when the pagan Roman emperor Constantine the Great was preparing to go into battle, he had a vision of a flaming cross in the sky with the words: "In this sign you shall conquer." He had the shields of his soldiers painted with a cross, won the battle, and made Christianity the official religion of the empire. He himself later became a Catholic.

The Sign of the Cross is the most frequently used sign in the Church. For most children, it is the first religious act they learn. It is a summary of Christian belief, the sign of our salvation. While you have made the Sign of the Cross hundreds of times, as a server it is very important that you do so reverently and thoughtfully.

Here is how to make the Sign of the Cross:
1. Begin with folded hands.
2. Place the left hand on your chest as you say:
3. *"In the name of the Father"* (with right hand straight, touch your forehead with the fingers of the right hand);
4. *"and of the Son"* (with your right hand touch your chest just above your left hand);
5. *"and of the Holy. . ."* (touch your fingers to your left shoulder);
6. *". . . Spirit."* (touch your right shoulder with the fingers of your right hand);
7. *"Amen."* (return your hands to the folded position).

The Sign of the Cross is made during Mass at the beginning of Mass after the entrance song, and during the blessing at the end of Mass.

Remember, the Sign of the Cross is not made if you are carrying something.

SMALL SIGN OF THE CROSS

The small Sign of the Cross is made at the announcement of the Gospel and follows the action of the priest or deacon. To make it, the right hand is closed loosely in a fist, thumb on top. The thumb traces the Sign of the Cross on the forehead, lips, and chest as we say "Glory to you, O Lord," in answer to the priest or deacon saying, "A reading from the holy Gospel...."

GENUFLECTIONS

The word "genuflection" comes from two Latin words: *genu*, knee; *flectere*, to bend. It means to touch the knee to the ground in worship. The custom of making a genuflection to show respect is very ancient and has existed among many different races of people. All Catholics are taught to genuflect to the Blessed Sacrament when entering and leaving church.

Rule: *If there is a tabernacle with the Blessed Sacrament in the sanctuary, a genuflection is made before and after Mass and whenever passing in front of the tabernacle outside of Mass.*

Rule: *The only exception to the rule on genuflections involves the cross-bearer who does not genuflect when carrying the processional cross, or the candle-bearers, who do not genuflect when carrying the candles.*

Rule: *On Good Friday, the exposed crucifix is given the same reverence as the-Blessed Sacrament.*

This is how a proper genuflection is made:

1. Genuflections always begin in a standing position facing the tabernacle. You do not genuflect while walking.

2. With hands folded, eyes looking at the tabernacle, bring your right leg back about half a step, then bend your right knee to the floor even with the heel of your left foot, body erect.

3. Pause briefly, then rise to the original standing position, feet together.

4. Proceed with the next action.

New servers should practice genuflections, particularly in their serving robes, so they will learn how to keep their balance and adjust their robes to prevent entanglement.

If the tabernacle is not in the sanctuary, bows to the altar may be substituted.

DOUBLE GENUFLECTIONS

A double genuflection, which is made before the exposed Blessed Sacrament, begins like the genuflection described above, except that after you kneel on your right knee, your left leg is brought back so that you are kneeling on both knees. Then a profound bow (see definition, Page 27) is made and then you stand up.

Double genuflections are generally no longer practiced.

BOWS

Bowing is a lesser form of reverence than genuflecting. There are two kinds of bows: a bow of the head (simple bow) and a bow of the body (profound bow).

Bow of the Head (or Simple Bow) — This bow is a slow nod. It is made when the Father, Son, and Holy Spirit are named together, and at the name of Jesus, Mary, or the saint in whose honor the Mass is celebrated.

Bows of the head are made whenever the server approaches or leaves the celebrant. For example, when bringing the wine and water, the servers approach the minister, stop when they reach him, bow their heads, and then proceed with the action.

The master of ceremonies may use a head bow as a cue for some action to begin.

Bow of the Body (or Profound Bow) — A body bow is made from the waist with hands folded. In this bow the shoulders and head are bent forward at about a 30-degree angle. It should be made slowly and reverently.

A body bow is made:

✠ Before the altar whenever the Blessed Sacrament is not present.

✠ During Mass whenever passing in front of the altar, even if the tabernacle is visible. The exceptions are genuflections to the tabernacle during the entrance and exit processions. This is because the altar takes priority during Mass itself.

✠ At the elevations of the consecration, if you are unable to kneel.

✠ In the Profession of Faith (Creed) at the words "and by the Holy Spirit was incarnate of the Virgin Mary, and became man." When several servers are bowing at the same time, care should be taken that the angle of the bow is the same for each.

WALKING

Walking should be done with grace and smoothness. When ministers are walking together, an impression of unison should be given. The pace should not be rushed but deliberate. Hands should be folded and the body not allowed to slouch. A good trick is to place one foot in front of the other — this will prevent "swaying" when walking in procession.

A cross-bearer or anyone who leads a procession must remember that he or she sets the pace for all.

When walking in pairs, act in unison, doing the same thing at the same time. When turning — for instance, after giving the minister the wine and water —

turn in toward each other, not away.

Steps often present a problem for new servers, and sometimes for older ones, especially if their serving robes are a bit too long. Many a server has exited blushing after tripping or stumbling. The trick when moving up steps is to lift the advancing leg higher than usual, set it down firmly on the step (not on the edge), and then repeat with the other foot.

CARRYING THE CROSS

A cross-bearer should be one of the taller servers who is better able to keep the cross balanced. The aim should be to carry the cross pole at a right angle to the floor and keep it from swaying in any direction.

Unless incense is used, the cross-bearer leads the procession, setting the pace for the whole group. It is best to be neither too slow nor too fast. *Practice helps a great deal.*

With the ordinary processional cross, the bottom of the pole should be about knee high. The right hand holds the pole about throat level and the left hand is placed about a foot below. The corpus (figure of Christ) always faces forward. When carrying the cross, the cross-bearer does not genuflect.

When the cross is not in use, it is best returned to the sacristy. If it is to remain in the sanctuary, a holder should be used. Placing a cross up against a wall is dangerous. Someone might trip over it or it could slip and fall with a loud crash.

CARRYING CANDLES

When the cross is carried in procession, there are usually two candle-bearers who walk on each side of the cross. Candle-bearers may also be used at the solemn singing of the Gospel and at other ceremonies. Since candle-bearers work in pairs, they should be matched in size so that candles will be held evenly.

Candles should be held at a right angle to the floor. It is important to keep them straight so that melted wax does not drip on the floor or carpet.

CARRYING THE MISSAL

You may be asked to hold up the Missal for the priest to read from at particular times during Mass, so that he can keep his hands free to extend in a gesture of prayer. Make sure that you hold it high enough for him to see, and keep the book still while he reads. Also, depending on your height relative to the priest's, you may want to stand to one side so you won't block his view of the people.

Make sure not to pull out the ribbons, which mark the prayers to be used that day!

SILENCE

Except for making the proper responses, silence is kept at all times. Nothing is more distracting to the priest or people than to see altar servers whispering together. Moreover, the arrangement of the liturgy is such that silence is observed at designated times as part of the celebration. At the Penitential Act, after the invitation to pray at the prayers, each should become recollected and join his thoughts to the minister's. After receiving Holy Communion, the server should praise God in his heart and pray.

SITTING

Sit erect with the palms of your hands flat against your legs and the edge of the fingers close to your knees.

STANDING

Do not slouch. Stand erect with hands properly folded. Heels should be separated slightly with the toes pointing somewhat to the sides.

A CAUTION

Because the postures at Mass are somewhat formal and a bit strange to us, individuals may at times become tense. This could possibly lead to feeling faint. If you should ever start to feel strange or faint, go immediately to the sacristy and sit down until you feel better.

Notes on Serving Mass at Your Parish

Each parish does things somewhat differently. This is because local customs vary and not all sanctuaries are set up exactly alike. So these next few pages are for you to take notes from your leader. This will help you to remember just how things are done in your parish. In the spaces provided write what the servers are to do during each of these moments of the Mass. Be sure to include all instructions for all the servers.

A. The Introductory Rites

*Entrance Procession:*_____

_____

*Greeting:*_____

_____

*Blessing and Sprinkling Holy Water:*_____

*Penitential Act:*_____

*Gloria:*_____

*Opening Prayer (Collect):*_____

B. The Liturgy of the Word

*First Reading, Responsorial Psalm, and Second Reading:*_____

*Gospel Acclamation:*_____

*Reading of the Gospel:*_____

*Homily:*_____

*Profession of Faith (Creed):*_____

*Prayer of the Faithful:*_____

C. The Liturgy of the Eucharist

*Preparation of the Gifts (Offertory):*_____

_____

*Eucharistic Prayer:*_____

_____

Communion Rite:
✠ Lord's Prayer (Our Father):_____

_____

✠ Sign of Peace:_____

_____

✠ *Agnus Dei* (Lamb of God):_____

_____

✠ Communion:_____

_____

✠ Prayer after Communion:_____

_____

D. The Concluding Rites

*The Final Blessing:*_____

_____

Dismissal and Recession: _____

_____

Prayers to Know

Y ou are already familiar with most of the prayers at Mass from having attended Mass for such a long time. We presume that you know the shorter ones. With the new English translation of the Mass, implemented in Advent 2011, there have been changes to the wording of many prayers. These are all good changes, making the prayers more beautiful and meaningful. But it is important to learn them well, so you can help lead the people at Mass. Your leader might quiz you on them just to be sure. The important thing to remember is that prayers are never mumbled. They are always said clearly and in a conversational tone. You don't need to shout so that you would be heard above the people, but you do have to be clear. Here are some of the longer prayers that you might wish to look over to be sure you know them accurately and well.

PENITENTIAL ACT

After the priest introduces the rite, one of three forms may be used, with the last form having a number of variations. When Form A is used, you will need to know the Confiteor (below). In all forms, you need to respond, "Lord have mercy" and "Christ, have mercy" — whenever the priest, deacon, or cantor sings or says these words.

CONFITEOR
(Priest, servers, and people)
I confess to almighty God,
and to you, my brothers and sisters,
that I have greatly sinned
in my thoughts and in my words,
in what I have done
and in what I have failed to do,
(All strike breast with closed right hand)
through my fault,
through my fault,
through my most grievous fault;
therefore I ask blessed Mary ever-Virgin,
all the angels and saints,
and you, my brothers and sisters,
to pray for me to the Lord our God.

The Gloria is sung or said on Sundays outside Advent and Lent and on solemnities and feasts. The servers should sing or say the Gloria in a firm voice, matching their cadence to that of the cantor or priest.

GLORIA

(Priest, servers, and people)
Glory to God in the highest,
and on earth peace to people of good will.
We praise you,
we bless you,
we adore you,
we glorify you,
we give you thanks for your great glory,
Lord God, heavenly King,
O God, almighty Father.
Lord Jesus Christ, Only Begotten Son,
Lord God, Lamb of God, Son of the Father,
you take away the sins of the world,
　　　have mercy on us;
you take away the sins of the world,
　　　receive our prayer;
you are seated at the right hand of the Father,
　　　have mercy on us.
For you alone are the Holy One,
you alone are the Lord,
you alone are the Most High,
Jesus Christ,
with the Holy Spirit,
in the glory of God the Father.
Amen.

On Sundays and solemnities the Profession of Faith (either the Nicene or Apostles' Creed) is recited or sung.

**PROFESSION
OF FAITH (CREED)**

(Priest, servers, and people)

NICENE CREED

I believe in one God,
the Father almighty,
maker of heaven and earth,
of all things visible and invisible.
I believe in one Lord Jesus Christ,

the Only Begotten Son of God,
born of the Father before all ages.
God from God, Light from Light,
true God from true God,
begotten, not made, consubstantial with the Father;
through him all things were made.
For us men and for our salvation
he came down from heaven,
(At the words that follow, up to and including
"and be came man," all bow.)
and by the Holy Spirit was incarnate
      of the Virgin Mary,
and became man.
For our sake he was crucified under Pontius Pilate,
he suffered death and was buried,
and rose again on the third day
in accordance with the Scriptures.
He ascended into heaven
and is seated at the right hand of the Father.
He will come again in glory
to judge the living and the dead
and his kingdom will have no end.
I believe in the Holy Spirit, the Lord, the giver of life,
who proceeds from the Father and the Son,
who with the Father and the Son is adored and glorified,
who has spoken through the prophets.
I believe in one, holy, catholic and apostolic Church.
I confess one Baptism for the forgiveness of sins
and I look forward to the resurrection of the dead
and the life of the world to come. Amen

APOSTLES' CREED   I believe in God,
the Father almighty,
Creator of heaven and earth,
and in Jesus Christ, his only Son, our Lord,
(At the words that follow, up to and including
"the Virgin Mary," all bow.)
who was conceived by the Holy Spirit,
born of the Virgin Mary,
suffered under Pontius Pilate,
was crucified, died and was buried;

he descended into hell;
on the third day he rose again from the dead;
he ascended into heaven,
and is seated at the right hand of God the Father almighty;
from there he will come to judge the living and the dead.
I believe in the Holy Spirit,
the holy catholic Church,
the communion of saints,
the forgiveness of sins,
the resurrection of the body,
and life everlasting. Amen.

Toward the end of the preparation of the gifts (offertory), the priest returns to the center of the altar and says:

(Priest)
Pray, brethren, that our sacrifice may be acceptable
to God, the almighty Father.

SUSCIPIAT   *(Servers, and people)*
DOMINUS   May the Lord accept the sacrifice at your hands
(MAY THE LORD   for the praise and glory of his name,
ACCEPT)   for our good and the good of all his holy Church.

After the preface, we sing or say together:

SANCTUS (HOLY,   *(Priest, servers, and people)*
HOLY, HOLY)   Holy, Holy, Holy Lord God of hosts.
Heaven and earth are full of your glory.
Hosanna in the highest.
Blessed is he who comes in the name of the Lord.
Hosanna in the highest

After the consecration, the priest sings or says:

The mystery of faith:

The servers and people respond with the acclamation as indicated by the priest or cantor:

MYSTERY   **A.** We proclaim your Death, O Lord,
OF FAITH   and profess your Resurrection
until you come again.

B. When we eat this Bread and drink this Cup,
we proclaim your Death, O Lord,
until you come again.
C. Save us, Savior of the world,
for by your Cross and Resurrection
you have set us free.

The priest introduces the Lord's Prayer.

LORD'S PRAYER
(OUR FATHER)

(Priest, servers, and people)
Our Father, who art in heaven,
hallowed be thy name;
thy kingdom come;
thy will be done on earth as it is in heaven.
Give us this day our daily bread;
and forgive us our trespasses
as we forgive those who trespass against us;
and lead us not into temptation,
but deliver us from evil.
(Priest)
Deliver us, Lord, etc.
(Servers)
For the kingdom, the power and the glory are
yours, now and forever.

AGNUS DEI
(LAMB OF GOD)

(Priest, servers, and people)
Lamb of God, you take away the sins of the world,
have mercy on us.
Lamb of God, you take away the sins of the world,
have mercy on us,
Lamb of God, you take away the sins of the world,
grant us peace.
(Priest)
Behold the Lamb of God,
behold him who takes away the sins of the world.
Blessed are those called to the supper of the Lamb.
(Servers/people)
Lord, I am not worthy
that you should enter under my roof,
but only say the word
and my soul shall be healed.

8 Celebrating the Year: The Seasons

The changing of the seasons in nature tells us many things. For those of us who live in a rural area, this is easy to see. In spring, we plant. In summer, we cultivate. In fall, we harvest. In winter, we wait, living on what has been stored up. But even in the city, where the closest we might come to food production is the local supermarket, we can feel the seasons. Spring is the time for coming out of the house, into the sunlight. Summer is a time for celebration and relaxation (and some work as well). In the fall, it's back to school to meet old and new friends. In winter, some of us bundle up and generally stay indoors; others brave the cold for skiing, sledding, and skating. As the seasons change, we change and grow. It's a continuing cycle.

The Church has seasons, too. Like the natural seasons, the seasons of the Church (called the liturgical seasons) keep repeating — over and over. But they never become old and tired. They're always fresh and new. Think of summer. Who gets tired of summer coming? We always get excited as it approaches. We look forward to it. Think of the Christmas season. It comes around every year, but it's always "new" for us. Why? The answer is that, while the season is the same, we are different, we are older. We've changed since the last time we celebrated the feast. So, every year we get something new out of it. We think of new things to do, new presents to give. We remember the old ways, those things that are traditional, but the celebration is always fresh and new.

The liturgical seasons are there to help us change, grow, and become closer to Christ. One of the clearest signs of these seasons is the changing liturgical colors. With each change of seasons, the Church changes the color of vestments as a visible sign of our need to change and grow. The colors used are:

White — Used in Masses of the Easter and Christmas seasons; on feasts and memorials of the Lord Jesus, other than Palm Sunday and Good Friday; on feasts and memorials of the Blessed Virgin Mary, the angels, saints who are not martyrs, All Saints (November 1), John the Baptist (June 24), John the Apostle (December 27), Chair of Peter (February 22), and Conversion of Paul (January 25). White is used on festive occasions (such as marriage and baptism) and is the usual color for Masses of the Dead. White is a sign of joy.

Red — Used on Passion Sunday and Good Friday, Pentecost, Masses of the

Holy Spirit, celebration of the Passion, feasts of the apostles and Evangelists, and feasts of martyrs. Red symbolizes the blood of Christ and martyrs, and the Holy Spirit.

Green — Used on the Sundays and weekdays of Ordinary Time. This color symbolizes growth and hope.

Violet — Used in Advent and Lent. It may be used in Masses of the Dead. It is a symbol of penance.

Rose — A color indicating joy. It may be used on Gaudete Sunday (Third Sunday of Advent) and Laetare Sunday (Fourth Sunday of Lent).

Gold — Substitutes for other colors and may be used on special feasts and occasions.

Black — May be used in Masses of the Dead, though it is no longer common.

On days when Votive Masses are permitted (indicated by a V in the Ordo), a color suited to the Mass itself or to the color of the day or season may be used. Masses for various occasions use the color of the day or season.

It's About Responsibility

Now that you are a server (or soon will be one), remember this: there are people counting on you. First, the priest depends on you. He needs to know that you will be there on time. He needs to know that you are prepared. You help him a great deal to ensure that things go smoothly. Remember, too, that the congregation counts on you. Without you, an important part of prayer leadership is missing. Without you, things can get sloppy. And no celebration of the Mass, or any prayer event, should be sloppy. A good server keeps things going smoothly.

No matter how well you are prepared, occasionally things go wrong. When something does go wrong, stay calm and just keep going. Quick movements are distracting and can lead to tripping and other troublesome mistakes. When there is a problem, think about it for a moment; then, if possible, do what is necessary to correct the problem.

Remember, be responsible. And be calm. You have been called to serve. Your parish is grateful that you have responded to this call with a real sense of dedication to service.

Appendix

PROCESSIONS

There are different types of processions in the Church. Some are prescribed by the liturgy, such as the procession on Palm Sunday. Others are for a special occasion, such as Corpus Christi. Still others are a more formal way of beginning a ceremony, such as a procession to the sanctuary for Sunday Mass.

Simple Procession

This is the ordinary entrance for some liturgical ceremonies — Mass, Benediction, special devotions. It is simply an orderly way to get from one place to another. The servers precede the minister in this procession. It may be the duty of one server to ring a bell announcing that the ceremony is about to begin.

The servers proceed before the altar. When the priest is in position, a bow (or genuflection if the Blessed Sacrament is reserved behind the altar) is made.

As the priest turns toward the people, the servers turn in toward the minister and accompany him to the altar of sacrifice where he will kiss it, then proceed to their usual place during Mass.

Then the procession goes to the presidential chair or customary spot where Mass will begin. It may be the custom for the servers to go immediately to the seats assigned them and stand facing the people, or it may be the custom for two servers, one on either side of the priest, to stand with him facing the people as he begins the opening prayers. If the latter is the case, the servers stand with the priest until he sits down. Then they bow to the priest and take their seats for the reading of Scripture.

More Formal Procession

This procession is usually made down the side aisle and up the center, although it may also be formed from the back of the church. It may consist of a cross-bearer and servers with candles. A deacon, lector, and cantor may also take part. The Book of the Gospels may be carried. According to the degree of solemnity desired, a thurifer and boat-bearer and other servers may be added.

Unless a thurifer leads the procession, the cross-bearer, flanked by servers with candles, leads the way. When the area directly before the altar is reached, the cross-bearer pauses while the servers accompanying him bow (or genuflect if the Blessed Sacrament is reserved behind the altar). The candles are extinguished, the cross put away, and they return to their place in the sanctuary for the start of Mass.

If, however, the candles are to be used at Mass, the cross-bearer goes alone to the place where the cross is kept. The candle-bearers place their candles where they are to be used at Mass and go to their places in the sanctuary.

Meanwhile, each row of the procession comes before the altar, genuflects, and goes to assigned places. The priest and deacon will kiss the altar after genuflecting.

On certain occasions, the "Rite of Blessing and Sprinkling Holy Water" may take place. This begins at the chair after the Mass has been introduced. It takes the place of the Penitential Act. A server with the water vessel comes forward and, after the prescribed prayer, accompanies the priest as he (the priest) sprinkles the people. The server is at the side of the priest and, at the end of the ceremony, takes the water vessel and aspergillum back to the sacristy.

Also on certain occasions, it may be the custom to incense the altar. If incense is to be used, the thurifer and boat-bearer, after genuflecting, separate and go around each side of the altar, and stand behind it to await the priest. When he arrives he will put incense in the thurible, take it, and incense the altar, accompanied by the thurifer, who follows his actions (if there is a deacon, he may accompany the priest around the altar). When the altar has been incensed, the two servers return their vessels to the sacristy, if appropriate, genuflecting to the Blessed Sacrament as they leave. Then they return to take their places in the sanctuary for Mass.

There is also a procession for the solemn singing/proclamation of the Gospel. This consists of two candle-bearers, a thurifer, a server who will hold the book, and the minister who will sing the Gospel. The servers with the candles lead the way to the left side of the ambo, standing to either side of it with candles held at equal heights. Here they pause and turn facing into the sanctuary. The server who will hold the book takes his or her place between them and receives the book from the minister, holding it at an angle before his face. The minister will bring the book to the ambo, incense it, then sing or proclaim the Gospel and take back the book. The minister with the book is then incensed. The candle-bearers and thurifer return to their place after the proclamation of the Gospel is completed, and before the homily.

INCENSATION

In the more solemn celebrations of the liturgy, incense is used. The custom of using incense in religious ceremonies is an ancient one. The Old Testament describes it as a rich perfume used in sacrifices and in Temple worship. Incense is a symbol of our recognition of God's majesty. It also symbolizes our prayer rising to God (see Psalm 141).

Two servers are used in incensing: (1) a thurifer who carries the thurible and has charge of it during the liturgical service; and (2) a boat-bearer who carries the incense to be used in the thurible.

The thurifer must arrive in the sacristy well in advance of the ceremony. It is his or her responsibility to light the charcoal and have it burning well in time for the ceremony. To keep the charcoal burning, he or she swings the thurible back and forth, evenly and carefully so as not to distract others.

Incense may be used (1) during the entrance procession, (2) for the incensation of the altar at the beginning of Mass, (3) in order to incense the Book of the Gospels before the proclamation of the Gospel, (4) to incense the gifts of bread and wine, the cross, the altar, the priest, and the congregation, (5) at the elevation of the Body and Blood of Christ.

Incense is also used at solemn Vespers, Benediction and in processions of the Blessed Sacrament.

Be aware that there are different kinds of thuribles — some with more chains or more complicated constructions than others. Make sure somebody trains you in how to use each particular thurible. Much practice is needed to become a very good thurifer.

Carrying the thurible

The thurible is carried with the right hand around the chain just below the top. It is carried to the side so that your knees do not hit it. It is swung gently back and forth to keep the charcoal burning. If it is swung too vigorously, there is the danger of sending hot coals flying or hitting someone near you. Your left hand is carried flat on your chest when you carry the thurible.

If there is no incense carrier, you will have to carry the boat in your left hand. If this is the case, you hand the boat to the minister at the time of preparing the incense.

If you are not tall enough to allow the thurible to hang naturally at your side, take the thurible by the chain just below the top in your left hand. Take the chain about a foot from the thurible in your right hand and with your right hand swing it at your side. Your left hand should be on your chest as it holds the top portion of the chain.

Carrying the boat

Walk at the left side of the thurifer in procession and whenever moving. Carry the boat with the cover closed in your right hand. When it is time for the incense to be used, go around behind the thurifer and stand at the minister's right hand. Open the boat and present it to the minister close to the open thurible so that incense grains will not fall to the floor. Be careful not to touch the hot thurible.

Presenting the thurible

As you approach the minister who will prepare the incense, transfer the thurible to your left hand. After a head (or simple) bow to the minister, raise the top of the thurible by pulling the chain about a foot. If there is a protective ring, this will have to be raised first.

With your right hand on the chain above the thurible lid, raise the thurible so that the minister can put in incense. Hold it raised for his blessing. Then close the lid and pass the thurible top to him. Do not touch the thurible itself, as it can get very hot and cause a burn.

Make a head bow before giving the thurible to and after receiving it back from the minister.

Incensing

Depending on the ceremony and the number of people taking part, you may have to incense the celebrant, other ministers, servers, people, Christ's Body and Blood at the elevations (while kneeling before the altar), or the Blessed Sacrament at Benediction (also while kneeling).

This is how you incense (practice this with an empty thurible):

(1) Transfer the end of the thurible chain to your left hand. (2) Take the chain of the thurible with your right hand about six inches above the thurible cup. Put your left hand on your chest. (3) Raise your right hand about chin high extended from your body, holding the chain as you would hold a pencil. (4) Use your wrist to make the number of swings required.

Swings

Swings should be made smoothly. There are two kinds of swings, and after each one a slight pause should be made. A single swing is done by swinging the thurible with the right hand from the chest, out to a full extension of the right arm and back. A double swing is done by swinging the thurible twice with the right wrist at the full extension of the single swing. Typically, servers will do double swings during Mass. Ask an experienced server or the priest to demonstrate different types of swings for you.

Here is how you render the number of swings:

✠ *Celebrant.* Three double swings, bowing with the head before and after. At Mass the celebrant is incensed after he has incensed the altar and before he washes his hands.

✠ *Concelebrants.* Three single swings, bowing with the body before and after.

✠ *Deacon.* Two double swings.

✠ *Servers.* Three single swings.

✠ *Congregation.* Three single swings — the first to the center, the second to your left, and the third to your right. The people are incensed from the front center of the sanctuary.

(The above incensations are made, in order, after the celebrant has been incensed during the preparation of the gifts. A head bow is made before and after each set. The boat-bearer does not accompany the thurifer during these incensations. When the incensing is finished, the thurifer returns to the rear center of the sanctuary, genuflects or bows, then joins the boat-bearer at the side of the sanctuary to await the elevation. At the conclusion of the *Sanctus*, the boat-bearer puts some incense in the thurible and the thurifer goes to the center, genuflects or bows, then turns and kneels before the altar. Candle-bearers often kneel alongside the thurifer. This action should be timed so that the thurifer is kneeling when the priest extends his hands over the offering.) While kneeling during the Eucharistic Prayer before and after the consecration, the thurifer should very gently swing the thurible from left to right in front of himself like a pendulum, to keep the coals burning.

✠ *Elevation.* During the Eucharistic Prayer, each elevation of the consecrated bread and wine is incensed with three double swings. After the Great Amen, the thurifer and candle-bearers may rise and stand before the Blessed Sacrament. When the boat-bearer joins you, you both genuflect and put the thurible and boat in their place. Return to your places in the sanctuary.

✠ *Benediction.* After the celebrant has incensed the Sacrament and returns the thurible to the thurifer, the thurifer rises and goes to kneel about three or four feet behind the celebrant. When the celebrant raises the Blessed Sacrament in blessing in the shape of the Sign of the Cross, the thurifer makes three double swings, once as the minister raises the monstrance on the up-and-down motion, once as he moves the monstrance to his left side, and once as he moves it to his right side. The thurifer remains kneeling in position until the Sacrament has been reposed.

Boat-bearer

In procession, standing, and kneeling, the boat-bearer is always at the left of the thurifer, whose lead he or she should follow. Carry the incense boat at the bottom in your left hand with the lid opening to the left. The spoon should point toward you. The right hand is held open against your chest.

When presenting the boat to the minister, make a head bow, open the cover, and lift the boat so that it is close to the bowl of the open thurible. After the incense has been transferred, make a head bow and step back several paces to await the thurifer. Remember that you and the thurifer are a team and that your actions should match whenever the thurifer is not actually incensing. Also be careful not to spill incense on the floor of the sanctuary.

At Mass you extend the incense boat to the minister: (1) behind the altar after the procession so that the altar may be incensed; (2) for the incensation before the proclamation of the Gospel; and (3) at the preparation of the gifts when the altar is again incensed. (You put incense in the thurible, which the thurifer will open before the consecration.)

Benediction. A server carries the incense boat at Benediction, offering it to the celebrant after the Sacrament has been exposed.

MASTER OF CEREMONIES

At more solemn celebrations, particularly if there are a large number of ministers and servers, a master of ceremonies may be used. It is his task to keep the ceremony flowing smoothly. He does this by giving cues through head bows at proper times. In order to do his job effectively, he must know the roles and responsibilities of those taking part in the ceremony. The master of ceremonies should not get in the way. His role is to assist the celebrant in carrying out the ritual of the Church.

There will almost always be a master of ceremonies assigned to episcopal Masses — that is, Masses with a bishop. When the bishop comes to visit a parish, it is a very special occasion. Altar servers asked to assist at an episcopal Mass should recognize it as a great honor, but also a serious responsibility. There are a number of special things that servers need to do during a Mass with the bishop (such as carry his crosier and miter). The master of ceremonies can help guide you in doing these things correctly.

OTHER CELEBRATIONS

During your ministry as a server, you will be called upon to assist at many different kinds of church celebrations other than the Mass. There will be baptisms, weddings, and funerals (usually celebrated within Mass), communal celebrations of penance, Benediction of the Blessed Sacrament, the Liturgy of the Hours, and various other kinds of celebrations to become familiar with.

The most important time of the year for your ministry will be Holy Week.

On Holy Thursday, Good Friday, and the Easter Vigil (these days are called the Triduum), you may feel that you are spending more time in church than out. But remember, these are the Church's highest holy days, and your service during these celebrations is very important. Pay very special attention to your duties during this time.

It would not be possible for us to give you directions for each celebration that will go on in your parish. It is therefore suggested that you get a notebook in which to write important notes about your part in the following events:

FUNERALS ✠ WEDDINGS ✠ BENEDICTION ✠ HOLY WEEK
CHRISTMAS ✠ NOTES OF SPECIAL INTEREST

ONE LAST RULE

BE PROMPT. Your leader will tell you how much in advance you will be expected to be in the sacristy to vest and prepare. *Be there on time.* Nothing disturbs a celebrant more than wondering, as time for Mass approaches, if he will have servers. Remember: for a server, to be early for Mass is to be on time to serve. So if you only arrive on time for Mass, it means you are late!

THANK YOU

Thank you for saying yes! Your parish is grateful for all you do to bring people closer to Christ by responding to his call to serve. May God bless you.